SPECTACULAR
NEW ZEALAND

Lake Middleton, Ohau

SPECTACULAR
NEW ZEALAND
THROUGH THE LENS OF MIKE HOLLMAN

TEXT BY SUE HALL

Hodder Moa

Devonport, North Shore, Auckland.

CONTENTS

The Information Centre, Rotorua.

The shore of Lake Taupo.

INTRODUCTION

New Zealand, an archipelago of three main islands in the South Pacific, is a relatively young country which has known human habitation for less than two thousand years. Pirouetting on the edge of two continental plates, its geology makes it a land of variety and contrast, a closely-knit canvas of snowy mountain ridges, forested valleys, rolling farmland and productive agricultural plains. It is resplendent with long sandy beaches, intimate coves, wild rocky coastlines and a vital maritime energy.

New Zealand's is a unique heritage. When the young country separated from its parent continent of Gondwanaland over 80 million years ago, it carried with it its own complement of plants and animals. Through subsequent millennia, ecosystems followed their own eccentric course and the disparate development of plants and animals evolved a distinct series of native species. The native forests rang to the birdsong of tui, bellbirds and kokako and, on the ground, giant moa pecked in the undergrowth and the flightless kiwi foraged in the night. Massive kauri, totara, rimu and miro trees reached for the skies above ferns, coprosmas, orchids, mosses and lichens and on the snowy mountain edges distinctive alpine plants learnt survival. A high percentage of the native plants and animals of present-day New Zealand are found nowhere else in the world. They are endemic, rare and often primitive.

Nelson by night.

Lake Ruataniwha, Canterbury.

When Maori journeyed from Polynesia to these southern islands, reputedly about AD1400, they named them Aotearoa, the 'land of the long white cloud'. Legend also told that Maui, standing in his canoe or waka (the South Island — Te Wai Pounamu — is long and narrow) fished up the North Island (Te Ika a Maui, the fish of Maui). Wellington is now located in the mouth of Te Ika. The Cape Reinga lighthouse is perched on its tail. Taranaki and East Cape are its fins. Rakiura, known as Stewart Island, is often referred to as the anchor to Maui's canoe.

Aotearoa was a land of plenty. The seashore offered a variety of seafoods, native pigeons were plump and juicy, inquisitive and easy to trap and moa were slow, ungainly and readily hunted as a source of meat and feathers for cloaks – they were eventually hunted to extinction. Tribal societies spread far around the North Island. A few lived in the south. Life was peaceful, abundant and rewarding – at least, until the arrival of marauding warriors from neighbouring or distant tribes.

This was the New Zealand that Captain Cook discovered for Europeans in 1769. By the mid 1800s Europeans were arriving in numbers with dreams of owning land and developing their rural Arcadia. New Zealand's forest mantle gradually slipped from its shoulders. Timber trees fell to resounding axe strokes and fires cleared land for agriculture. Thus began the inexorable changes that made New Zealand what it is today, a land of dairy, beef and sheep farms, orchards, cropping and vineyards, large forested national parks and small and large town and city centres. Export products are largely agricultural, but manufacturing enterprises are diversifying and displaying the ingenuity of a vibrant and explorative economy. Crowds on city footpaths demonstrate an increasingly multicultural society.

The national population of New Zealand is just over 4 million, over 1.4 million live in Auckland, 75 per cent live in the North Island, 90 per cent live within 40 kilometres of the coast and the overall population density is about 15 people per square kilometre.

REGIONS OF NEW ZEALAND

NORTHLAND · Whangarei

AUCKLAND · Auckland

Hamilton · Tauranga

WAIKATO · Whakatane

BAY OF PLENTY

EAST CAPE

Taupo · Gisborne

New Plymouth

Volcanic Plateau

TARANAKI

HAWKE'S BAY

MANAWATU & WANGANUI · Napier

Wanganui

Palmerston North

Masterton

WELLINGTON & WAIRARAPA

NELSON · Nelson

Wellington

TASMAN · Blenheim

MALBOROUGH

Greymouth

WEST COAST

Southern Alps

Christchurch

CANTERBURY

Ashburton

Timaru

Oamaru

OTAGO

SOUTH LAND · Dunedin

Invercargill

The lighthouse at Cape Reinga.

Sandboarding near Te Paki Stream, Ninety Mile Beach.

NORTHLAND

At the far north of New Zealand the land narrows to a long peninsula — the tail of the legendary Te Ika a Maui — and on its very tip perches the Cape Reinga lighthouse. Below is a turmoil of water where the great Pacific Ocean meets the Tasman Sea, a boiling pot of colliding waves that sometimes, when a big swell runs, are flung over 10 metres high. This is a magical place where the universe seems larger, where distances are dreamed of and ocean fills the senses. For Maori it is the mystical place from which departing spirits leave for the afterworld.

To reach it one must pass through Northland and, on the way, make difficult choices from a myriad of destinations, attractive for their scenic beauty, natural or historical interest. The far north, with its sub-tropical climate, is a land of isolated beaches, sun and aquatic beauty, boasting some of the best fishing and diving waters in the world. At Ninety Mile Beach the sand seems to stretch forever, dotted with hardy fisherfolk keen to haul in 'the big one'. From Taipa through to Coopers Beach, Mangonui and Matauri Bay, holiday homes, camping grounds, apartments and an international hotel and conference centre are testament to the area's attraction for tourists. Indented sandy bays fringed with pohutukawa trees, rocky edges, open rolling waves and offshore islands create panoramas that take the breath away. Inland, on more isolated roads, settlements are dotted amongst forest and farmland.

The waterfront at Russell, Bay of Islands.

The Treaty House at Waitangi, Bay of Islands.

On the west coast, the Hokianga, as we call the land surrounding the Hokianga Harbour, is a gem of quiet rural and coastal placidity. Along the waterfronts small towns lead the quiet life, welcoming passing travellers and offering transport by vehicular ferry across the harbour. Other communities, often centred around a Maori marae, are hidden in the hills or on remote coastal edges. The long indented harbour had long been a haven for waka, sailing, fishing and trading vessels. Now it is a quiet backwater used mainly by local fishermen, kayakers and pleasure boats. Further south is the Waipoua Forest which guards the largest kauri trees left in New Zealand. Tane Mahuta, the largest, is 51 metres high and has a girth of over 13 metres.

Another haven for sailors is on the eastern side of Northland. When Europeans first arrived in the beautiful Bay of Islands it was well-established with thriving kainga (villages). So appealing was the area to early European whalers, settlers and missionaries that it became the hub of trade, negotiation and government. At Waitangi, in 1840, the founding document of New Zealand nationhood, the Treaty

LEFT: Paihia, Bay of Islands.

Detail of the Waka House which houses the 35.7-metre war canoe Ngatokimatawhaorua in the Waitangi Treaty House grounds.

The Stone Store at Kerikeri, Bay of Islands.

A misty Northland morning.

of Waitangi, was signed and Kororareka, now Russell, became New Zealand's first seat of government.

Today, the Bay of Islands bustles with leisure activity. Passenger ferries ply the water between Paihia and Russell and a vehicular ferry makes the link from Opua. The enchanting beauty of 144 green islands set within a far-reaching harbour of secluded bays, rocky outcrops and blue water has spawned a thriving tourist economy. In the main towns quaint colonial buildings and historic sites attract visitors. On the water the sun entices fisherfolk, pleasure trippers and divers and, in all weathers, the occasional giant luxury cruise ship.

At the end of one of the bay's inlets lies Kerikeri, today a burgeoning town known for its orchards and art. New Zealand's oldest house, the Kerikeri Mission House (1821) and the Stone Store (1832) still stand by the languid waters of the upper inlet.

Whangarei, also sited at the headwaters of a beautiful harbour, is Northland's only city. Remote from the city and opposite the craggy mountains of the Whangarei Heads is Marsden Point, the major port of the north.

RIGHT: Quayside at the Town Basin, Whangarei.

Vineyard at Matakana, North Auckland.

Waiwera, North Auckland.

The Auckland Art Gallery.

Sandspit, North Auckland.

Cheltenham Beach, North Shore.

AUCKLAND

Auckland, the 'City of Sails' and New Zealand's largest city, spreads its urban growth over an isthmus between two harbours and over a northern shore along the stunningly beautiful Hauraki Gulf — an island playground for boaties, yachties and walkers. The isthmus is studded with volcanic cones, most of which are parks and historical reserves set aside as magnificent vantage points from which to view the city and sea. Rangitoto Island, a black lava volcano only 600 years old and covered with the country's largest pohutukawa forest, forms an iconic sentinel at the entrance to the Waitemata Harbour.

The 40 or so islands of the Hauraki Gulf are spread wide and have traditionally provided residential and holiday accommodation and farming opportunities. Now several have been designated as nature reserves. Tiritiri Matangi Island is a recently reforested island sanctuary where the general public can hear the birdsong of yesteryear. Little Barrier Island has long been a bird and plant sanctuary where access is only possible through permit.

Great Barrier Island, a sprawling forested island about half the size of metropolitan Auckland, is the largest and most distant in the gulf. It is a haven of peace and tranquillity, wilderness and rare birdlife. The mainly farming-based population of about 1100, spread in small settlements around the coast, pride themselves on their laid-back, simple lifestyle.

Kawau Island, by contrast, developed a very individual character when Sir George Grey (1812–1898),

Rangitoto Island, Waitemata Harbour

Fountain at Mission Bay, Auckland City.

Auckland CBD through morning mist.

Governor of New Zealand, bought it as his home. There, he extended a copper-mine manager's house into what is today called Mansion House and transformed the island into a private kingdom complete with a farm and a community of about 100. As a keen naturalist he introduced exotic animals and planted some fine specimens of exotic plants and trees.

Not all islands have escaped Auckland's urban sprawl. Waiheke Island, much closer in, has become one of its dormitory suburbs, vibrant with commercial activity, restaurants, wineries, olive groves, popular beaches and art and craft markets. As it can be reached from several parts of the city within 35 minutes by ferry, many people live on the island and commute to the mainland for work.

The CBD of Auckland, the business hub of the nation, is an iconic city centre where tall tower buildings overlook an energetic harbour and passenger and container wharves. The Auckland Harbour Bridge links the city to the North Shore, itself a city in its own right, one of the four that make up Greater Auckland (Auckland City, North Shore City, Manukau City and Waitakere City). Across the Waitemata

Auckland Harbour Bridge.

RIGHT: Gannet colony at Muriwai, West Auckland.

Harbour, only 10 minutes by ferry from the downtown Ferry Building, is Devonport, a suburb steeped in history, a quaint old harbourside township of restaurants, bookstores, clothing and art stores nestled amongst fine examples of Victorian villas and sprawling bungalows.

Out east of Auckland, and south alongside the Manukau Harbour, newer suburbs are expanding and developing, reflecting the increasingly multicultural nature of the city. The international airport at Mangere brings more immigrants every day. Now, with a population of over 1.2 million, Auckland's patterns of residential housing are changing as infill-housing breaks up the former 'quarter-acre section' and apartment blocks rise high within the city rim.

Not far from the madding crowds though, within and beyond the Waitakere Ranges, nature still holds sway. Along the west coast, forested valleys run down to wild black-sand beaches, and the wind-whipped waves of the Tasman Sea pound onto cliffs and shore. A natural wonderland of native plants and animals, seashore and rock life abounds.

Bethell's Beach (Te Henga), West Auckland.

Preece Point, Coromandel Peninsula.

Hot Water Beach, Coromandel Peninsula.

Cathedral Cove, Coromandel Peninsula.

WAIKATO, KING COUNTRY AND COROMANDEL

On the lush alluvial plains of the Waikato River and in the Piako and Hauraki Plains districts — the former Waikato riverbed — dairy farmers green up the countryside. Fodder crops of maize or grass for silage and hay, forage crops of turnips or brassicas and the odd cash crop of asparagus, change slightly the texture of continuous grass paddocks. Dairy cattle amble along the race to the milking shed once or twice a day. Cattle dogs and farmers on motorbikes help them on their way.

All the small towns dotted evenly about the region, and the city of Hamilton, have their origins as service centres to the farming industry. On the Te Rapa 'Straight', the main road leading north from Hamilton through the industrial suburbs, rows of businesses sell tractors, silage wagons, diggers, tedders, trailers, disc-ploughs or seed drills. The city centre developed alongside the Waikato River and a variety of architectural bridges span the waters and tree-lined banks to reach the residential suburbs. Cambridge, not far away and

The iconic Lemon & Paeroa bottle at Paeroa.

in the heart of an affluent farming and horse stud region, is renowned for its picturesque old-world English heritage and architecture, trees and shady walkways.

The mighty Waikato River, the longest in New Zealand, has a catchment equal to 12 per cent of the area of the North Island as it carves its way through 425 kilometres from Lake Taupo to the west coast at Port Waikato. Some of its tributaries originate in the westward rolling limestone hills around Otorohanga and Waitomo. Here, dairying gives way to dairy beef, beef and a few sheep. Underground, water runs through tomo caves and at Waitomo township visitors can journey underground into limestone 'cathedrals' full of glowworms, stalactites and stalagmites. Black-water rafting also thrills the more adventurous.

The Coromandel Peninsula, to the north-east of the Waikato region, is a natural wilderness gem where a central forested mountain ridge runs down on both sides to a variety of beautiful beaches, secluded rocky or sandy bays and scattered small townships. Roads on the west coast wind along the rocky edge of the Firth of Thames, with pohutukawa

St Andrews Church, Cambridge.

A typical Waikato scene.

The Fairfield Bridge, Hamilton.

LEFT: Annual Balloon Festival, Hamilton.

Rowing on Lake Karapiro.

Raglan on the Waikato west coast.

BELOW: Sunrise over the Waikato countryside.

trees clinging to the coastal strip and leaning up over the road. Offshore, where small islands abound, the reefs and surrounding seas are bountiful to local fishermen, oyster and mussel farmers. Along the rugged coast north of Thames, a town built on fishing and gold mining within the nearby hills, holiday baches nestle in quiet bays. Coromandel Town, settled into the arm of a harbour, is the town centre for a thriving community of artists and alternative lifestylers.

On the eastern side of the peninsula where the Pacific Ocean rolls to shore there are long languid sandy beaches which sometimes whip to a fury of waves that delight droves of surfers. Larger towns and holiday communities such as Pauanui come alive in summer, favourite haunts for families, swimmers and boaties. People are drawn to the hot springs on the sands of Hot Water Beach. Offshore, the Mercury Islands and Alderman Islands draw boaties 15 to 20 kilometres over a blue sea.

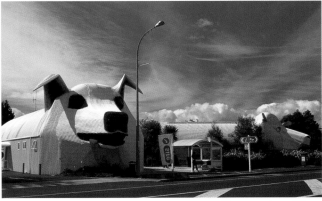

The township of Tirau.

Whanganui River at Taumarunui.

The Huka Falls, north of Taupo.

BELOW: A view across Lake Taupo.

A natural hot spring, near Taupo.

THE VOLCANIC PLATEAU

Strange darkness and lights were seen in the skies of Ancient Rome and China when in AD186 a cataclysmic explosion threw 80 cubic kilometres of ash and boiling rock into the air in the central North Island of New Zealand. When the ash settled, it surrounded a series of craters covering 616 square kilometres. Over time these filled with rainwater and became what is, today, beautiful Lake Taupo, New Zealand's largest lake.

Luxury accommodation and trees line the lake, a playground for water sports and trout fishing. The huge lake provides for almost any aquatic sport — apart from surfing! On its banks, Taupo town is the scenic focal point for anyone wanting to explore the natural wonders of the Volcanic Plateau, ski on nearby mountains, fish mountain rivers, or tramp or hunt in nearby forests.

The town lies alongside the Lake Taupo outflow, the headwaters of the mighty Waikato River, and a short distance north, the river waters tumble dramatically over the Huka Falls, at a rate of 220,000 litres per second. A rolling roar attracts plenty of sightseers and several thrill-seekers who join a jet-boat trip to the face of the falls. So much water flows into the Waikato River that it is able to feed nine or so hydro power stations

on its downward path. Each power-station dam forms a lake and many are used for recreational purposes, such as Lake Karapiro, scene of many national and international rowing competitions.

Geothermal activity is evident in much of the Volcanic Plateau and, in places, often on the side of the road, wisps of steam rise from the ground where underground water is heated by magma close to the surface. At Wairakei geothermal station the steam is released and harnessed to run turbines.

The roads to the south lead into the highlands of the plateau. Here, soft tussock country is cut into ravines by water flowing from three volcanic mountains, Tongariro, Ngauruhoe and Ruapehu, so high that their tops are covered in snow for a large part of the year. Mount Ruapehu is a favoured destination for skiers from all over the country and globe. Ski fields are accessed from the west at Whakapapa and the south-west from Ohakune. Between the Ruahines and Tongariro National Park, this small town of Ohakune is the accommodation centre of a thriving tourist attraction at Turoa, a ski field on the southern slopes of Ruapehu.

Mind that kiwi! Tongariro National Park.

The Chateau with Mt Ruapehu in the background.

Mt Ruapehu erupts, 1995.

The famous Ohakune carrot.

Surrounding market gardens have made Ohakune the 'carrot capital' of the country.

The Tongariro Crossing is an internationally popular walking track that passes alongside the mountain-top Red Crater, Emerald Lakes and Blue Lake — in summer, a moon-like dry landscape where trampers are stunned by spectacular volcanic features and rich colours and sweeping views over the Desert Road and forested mountains beyond.

Ruapehu burst its way onto national newspapers in 1995 and 1996 when it sent up showers of ash which covered and closed the ski fields on its flanks. The sleeping giant is monitored daily to protect the hordes of visitors who returned to its natural attractions.

A much older story told by Ngati Tuwharetoa relates how their ancestor, Ngatoroirangi, was close to death after climbing Tongariro. He called out to his sisters in the Pacific homeland of Hawaiki to send him fire to keep him warm. The fire came, but underground, forcing its way to the surface at Whakaari (White Island), Rotorua and Tokaanu before it reached their brother on the mountain.

Beach front and 'the Mount', Mt Maunganui.

The big kiwifruit of Te Puke.

Bay of Plenty and East Cape

For iconic sandy beaches lined with pohutukawa — the scarlet-flowering coastal tree that New Zealanders call their 'Christmas tree' — the Bay of Plenty and East Cape are the places to visit. Eighteenth-century explorer Captain James Cook was so impressed with the vegetation, food resources and the welcome he received from local Maori in the Bay of Plenty that he named it accordingly.

Today, the city of Tauranga, commercial hub of the Bay of Plenty, thrives in the same way. A major port, it is the cargo gateway for logs, woodchip, dairy products, kiwifruit and other primary products that are grown in the hinterland. The attractive city has spread around the coastal edge and is now linked to Mount Maunganui by a bridge which crosses a picturesque tidal lagoon between the two. Mount Maunganui is a magnet to young summer crowds, board-riders and swimmers. Its long white sandy beach is only one of the many around the bay.

Inland from here, Rotorua City is the gateway to a thermal wonderland. Mud pools boil brown and oozing, geysers perform sky-reaching spectacles and sulphur lakes steam in radiant colours. Visitors can luxuriate in thermal mineral springs. Traditionally Maori made good use of the bounties of hot water and

The Bath House in Government Gardens, Rotorua.

A thermal mud pool, Rotorua.

air for cooking and for body warmth. Today, many in Rotorua provide cultural displays of traditional dance, song and hangi (cooking). So much in the city is designed to welcome visitors to share in its wonders — luxury accommodation, simple accommodation, motels by the hundreds and a variety of restaurants and cultural centres.

The landscape on the outskirts of the city provides a marvel land of beautiful lakes famous for their blue and green colour, trout and tourist-boat services. Lake Tarawera is at the foot of spectacular Mount Tarawera whose long gashed crater draws trampers keen to see its remote sacred terrain. It was an eruption from here in 1886 that destroyed the world-famous Pink and White Terraces.

From Rotorua, the road to East Cape passes by Whakatane, a pretty town of about 16,800 people, sited at a river mouth and under the lee of a huge bluff that rises from the sea in the eastern Bay of Plenty. Forty-eight kilometres offshore, White Island (Whakaari, as Maori named it) sits on the horizon. The island is an active volcano and private scenic reserve, accessible with licensed boat and helicopter operators. It is

LEFT: Sunset on Lake Rotorua.

A geyser erupts at Whakarewarewa, Rotorua.

Lake Tarawera, near Rotorua.

Te Ara ki te Tairawhiti (the Pathway to the Sunrise), Opotiki.

Sunrise in Whakatane.

BELOW: Sunset at Waiotahi Beach, Opotiki.

Church at Raukokore, East Cape

East Cape, Eastland.

Young Nick's Head, Poverty Bay.

possible to walk inside the main crater, just above sea level, amongst steam and sulphur fumeroles.

Thick native forest stands untouched in the Urewera, the backbone ridge of the East Cape. It and the foreshore are the lifeblood of the many small, mainly Maori, communities that live around the bays and along river banks of the Cape. Remote from main centres, people here lead a quiet life, retaining their culture and traditions. Te reo (the Maori language) is spoken freely and fluently. Walking tracks go deep into the forest. At Waikaremoana 'lake of rippling waters', a Great Walks walking track circumnavigates the lake.

The main city of the region is in Poverty Bay — again, named by Captain Cook — although it is far from impoverished today. Gisborne, the first city in the world to see the sun each day, is the commercial and cultural hub the southern East Cape. The fertile alluvial plains support intensive farming of market-garden produce and sub-tropical fruits. Grapes here are the fresh-to-press backbone of a strong winemaking industry famous for its Chardonnay and, more recently, aromatic Gewürztraminers.

BELOW: Tolaga Bay, Eastland.

Wainui Beach, Gisborne.

Wreck of the *Gairloch*, Weld Rd Beach, Taranaki.

BELOW: Moonrise, Mt Taranaki and the Cape Egmont Lighthouse.

TARANAKI AND MANAWATU-WANGANUI

These regions stretch from the Taranaki Plains — a ring of green surrounding a majestic mountain — through undulating and deeply-gorged national park forest and sheep and beef country through which the Whanganui River flows, to the Manawatu and Rangitikei Plains, cut deep by river ravines originating in the long ridges of the Tararua Ranges.

State Highway 45, which curves around the rugged magnificent coast of Taranaki, is often called Surf Highway 45, for good reason. Inland, 2700 dairy farms generate 26 per cent of New Zealand's dairy production. New Plymouth, Taranaki's major city and the only deep-water port on New Zealand's west coast, is the base for New Zealand's major oil, gas and petrochemical industries. It is also famous for its parks and gardens.

From coast or dairy farm, town or city, or from the air, the dominant feature of Taranaki is Mount Taranaki/Egmont, a grand, snow-topped forest-clad circular cone in a sea of green farms, rising to 2518 metres.

The Windwand, New Plymouth.

A circular walking track navigates the sub-alpine forest ring and several tracks head upwards to the snow. Ski fields have been developed on the eastern slopes.

Starting from rain- and snow-water run-off from the flanks of Mt Tongariro, the Whanganui River gathers water and momentum as it runs south through the Whanganui National Park eastwards of Taranaki. It is a favourite of canoeists and kayakers eager to savour the mature podocarp forest and bird-life along its banks, its exciting low-grade rapids, sheer cliffs of river gorges and a vital Maori cultural presence. It meets the coast beside the city of Wanganui, a pretty coastal and river community of heritage buildings, light and heavy manufacturing and farm service which, in the 1900s, built up the reputation of being the gateway to the 'Rhine of New Zealand'.

Maori legend tells us that the mountains Tongariro and Taranaki, then both in the central plateau, became locked in furious conflict over their love for the small nearby mountain, Pihanga. Eventually a mighty battle ensued, won by Tongariro. Taranaki in furious despair, wrenched himself from the ground and tore a path through the country towards

Taranaki countryside.

RIGHT: The Fernery at Pukekura Park, New Plymouth.

Old store, Otakeho.

Tunnel to Durie Hill elevator, Wanganui.

The *Waimarie*, Whanganui River, Wanganui.

the setting sun. On reaching the coast he turned north and came to rest in the plains of Taranaki. Water soon gathered to heal the wound he had created in the earth, forests grew and birdsong filled the air. Thus, the Whanganui River was born.

Further south, the broad Rangitikei and Manawatu Plains are girded on the east by the Ruahine and Tararua Ranges. Snow-clad in winter, the high Tararua Ranges provide a rain-shadow effect over the agricultural plains, making sure they are well watered. Wind farms in the foothills supplement the electricity supply for local towns and the city of Palmerston North. 'Palmy', as the city is called by the many students who attend universities there, is the site of the Linton Military Camp and various research institutes.

There is only one main road between the Ruahine and Tararua Ranges, and that's through the Manawatu Gorge, a dramatic winding wilderness road of great beauty. Through the other side is Dannevirke, a town that originated in 1872, developed by 13 Danish and eight Norwegian families intent on a new life. As well as being a service centre it is frequently visited for its Viking heritage.

Ansett House, Palmerston North.

Sarjeant Gallery, Wanganui.

Te Apiti Wind Farm, Manawatu.

Raukawa Falls, Whanganui River.

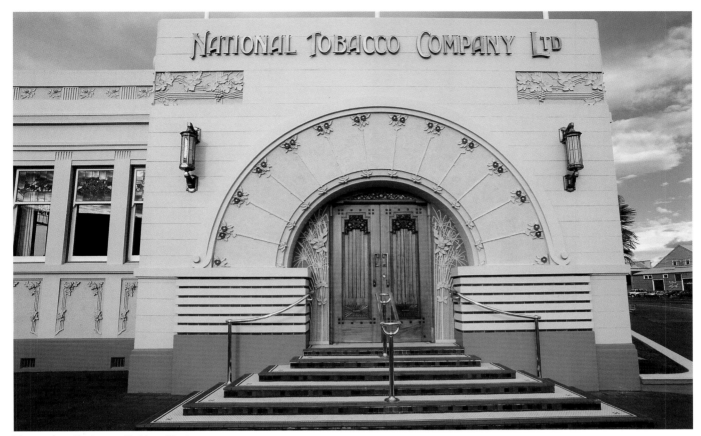

The art deco Rothmans Building, Napier.

HAWKE'S BAY

Hawke's Bay is an epicurean's playground of spontaneous delights. Nicknamed 'the fruit bowl of New Zealand', its long sunshine hours make it an ideal region for orchards, vineyards, market gardens and al fresco dining. No matter what the season, plenty is 'in season', from new asparagus, lettuce, strawberries and herbs in spring to eggplant, sweetcorn, cherries, berries and stone fruit in summer. Autumn brings on apples, pears, avocados, olives and citrus, and, in winter, indoor diners tuck in to hearty vegetables. All year round, award-winning wineries offer their visceral wares and complementary restaurant fare.

From Te Mata Peak (399 metres), in the south of the region — a favoured destination for walkers, rock climbers, paragliders and hang-gliders — uninterrupted views sweep the length of Hawke Bay, overlook the main cities of Napier and Hastings, the verdant alluvial plains and west to the Ruahine, Kaweka and Maungaharuru mountain ranges with Ruapehu in the background. Protected from westerly winds, Hawke's Bay region is warm and welcoming. Swimmers and surfers swarm to the sandy and/or pebbly coast, fisherfolk flock to internationally-rated trout rivers and on the Marine Parade of Napier City, children can visit leisure parks or the National Aquarium or play with dolphins in a marine park.

Napier has a unique beauty and is renowned as the 'Art Deco Capital of the World'. After a devastating earthquake in 1931 the entire town centre was rebuilt, mostly in the art deco style of the time. Nowhere

LEFT: Tom Parker Fountain, Napier.

The Daily Telegraph Building, Napier.

else in the world is there such a variety or concentration of art deco motif. And Napier residents love it. Art deco and earthquake tours proudly show off the city's heritage, and in summer and winter festivals many of the locals dress in art deco fashion. Hastings too, less than 20 kilometres away, was badly affected by the quake and, in rebuilding, also turned a new face to the world, much of it in the Spanish Mission style.

Mission Estate, established in 1851 by the French Marist religious order to make sacramental and red table wines, is New Zealand's oldest winemaker. It is now only one of about 55 wineries centred around Napier, Hastings and Havelock North. Chardonnay is the most widely planted grape variety but varied soil types and the long sunshine hours attract several later-ripening red grape varieties such as Merlot, Cabernet Sauvignon, Syrah and Cabernet Franc.

A history of looking after what grows in the soil is complemented by care for the waters and biodiversity of the bay. North of Napier, Boundary Stream Scenic Reserve is a mainland island dedicated to the restoration of bird

Spirit of Napier statue, Napier.

species such as native pigeon, tui, bellbird, rifleman, fantail, whitehead, silvereye, grey warbler, morepork and kaka. Robin, kiwi, saddleback and kokako have recently been introduced. At river mouths care is being taken to ensure the survival of natural fish nurseries, and popular fishing rivers are restocked with trout.

At Cape Kidnappers, the southernmost point of Hawke Bay, the world's largest and most accessible mainland gannet colony draws bird lovers from far and wide. These colourful white birds, known as takapu to Maori, from a distance form a huge white splash of activity encompassing almost the whole of a plateau near the tip of the cape. Up close, visitors can observe their intimate domestic arrangements — but they, too, value their privacy.

One of Hawke's Bay's many vineyards.

The Tukituki Valley.

Te Mata Peak.

The Martinborough Hotel.

BELOW: Martinborough countryside.

WELLINGTON AND WAIRARAPA

Wellington has lost its image of being a hill-bound city of wind, a cable car and nobody but politicians. Now, the close-knit intimate streets hum with delightfully cosmopolitan restaurants and cafés, and relaxed foreshore crowds have to choose amongst up-market shops, restaurants, museums (Te Papa, the national museum and the Museum of Wellington, City and Sea are here), libraries, theatre, fine arts or a stroll along smartly residential Oriental Parade. Looking inland from the harbour, Parliament Buildings and the quirky Beehive (government executive offices) are dwarfed by the brightly-renovated Victorian villas terraced up the surrounding hillsides.

Satellite suburbs spread early from the young city, north to the Hutt Valley and westwards towards the coast and, Upper Hutt, Lower Hutt and Porirua are now cities in their own right. Further north up the Kapiti Coast several evenly-spaced towns take full advantage of the beautiful coast, sheltered from the south by the massive Tararua Ranges, all easily linked to Wellington City by road and rail. Offshore, Kapiti Island is a sanctuary playing a major part in saving numerous threatened bird species and the adjacent Kapiti Island Marine Reserve is helping to restore a depleted fishery.

Te Papa, Museum of New Zealand, Wellington City.

The Beehive, Wellington City.

Walkways around the harbour edge open up wild and varied terrain. The dramatic Rimutaka Range north of the city is squeezed and faulted into a ridge separating the city from the Wairarapa lowlands. Geologically it is a volatile area, the land being under pressure where the Pacific and Indo-Australian continental plates collide. The biggest known earthquake in New Zealand was the Wairarapa earthquake of 1855, estimated at 8.2 on the Richter scale, which caused a vertical shift of 5000 square kilometres of land from 0 to 6.4 metres and in some places, horizontally up to 12 metres. With only sparse settlement of mainly sheep farmers at the time, the death toll reached five.

The shortest way to the Wairarapa is through the Rimutakas and, in the weekend, the road is abuzz with leisure-seeking Wellingtonians heading for Wairarapa's main town of Masterton and beyond, or to the small creative country towns of Carterton, Greytown and Martinborough — world-renowned for its exceptional Pinot Noirs.

The Wairarapa is also the gateway to many winding no-exit roads that traverse the eastern farming hill country to stunning bays on an isolated coast — bays where rock patterns show eons of shifting strata. At magnificent Castlepoint, fossil-encrusted rock has been thrust up to protect an inner sandy lagoon from the awesome battering of ocean waves. Just north, at Mataikona, pinnacles of rock stand sentinel over isolated beaches of pebbles of myriad hues and patterns.

South from Martinborough is the road past Lake Ferry around Palliser Bay, another coast road with dramatic scenery. It passes the spectacular Putangirua Pinnacles and winds through quirky Ngawi, a fishing township where bulldozers and trailers line the beach ready to pluck returning fishing boats from the surf. Further east, the Te Kawakawa rocks stand on the foreshore, sacred to Maori and a living part of legends created in the earliest occupation sites recorded in New Zealand. At the end of the road is Cape Palliser, the south-eastern tip of the North Island and home to the island's only well-established breeding colony of fur seals. Up 252 steps, the automated Cape Palliser lighthouse affords magnificent views both north and south, and is an essential tool for coastal and Cook Strait traffic.

Oriental Parade, Wellington City.

The Wellington Cable Car climbs above the city.

Mural, Wellington City.

Surfers at Lyall Bay.

Looking towards Kahurangi National Park from Takaka Hill.

NELSON AND MARLBOROUGH

A map readily shows how spectacularly varied and beautiful the northern coast of the South Island is. Fingers of forested and farmed land sprawl steeply into bays and waterways of the sounds. Extensive curved sand beaches nestle within the protective arm of Farewell Spit.

The large interisland ferries that carry passengers, cars, trucks and trains across Cook Strait from Wellington to Picton, pass through the sparkling waterways of the Marlborough Sounds, a stunning visual medley of islands, forested ridges, rocky cliffs, coastal breaking water, seabird and fish life. Its tranquil sandy coves like Governors Bay, Ponga Cove, Mistletoe Bay, Penguin Cove and Ship Cove are peaceful hideaways for bach and boat owners and holidaymakers. In the headwaters of Queen Charlotte Sound a former lodging house at Anakiwa was converted in 1962 into an outdoor pursuit centre. Many a New Zealander and foreigner has enjoyed its challenging physical courses designed to stimulate self-awareness, empathy and confidence.

Not many travellers however, could stay overlong in this natural haven without wanting to foray further south to the Blenheim district. Wine is the attraction: wine, wine and more wine. Marlborough is the largest

LEFT: Kaiteriteri Beach.

Split Apple Rock, Tasman Bay.

winegrowing region in the country with over 3000 hectares of vineyards. A wine trail through the hills and river valleys explores sparkling and still wines, including Sauvignon Blanc, Chardonnay, Reisling, Pinot Noir, Pinot Gris, Viognier, Cabernet Sauvignon and Merlot. Each February the Marlborough Wine Festival showcases the region's bounty, drawing people from all over the world. Each year overseas winemakers try to find the secrets to bettering the Marlborough Sauvignon Blancs!

A westerly turn on the road from Picton heads through the Richmond Range to the city of Nelson. Here, real estate in the hills behind the historic settlement has been expanding rapidly in recent years. Little wonder, as the views are spectacular, across city beaches and estuaries — bounded by a 15-kilometre-long boulder bank — and out into the mighty Tasman Bay, past the wine and fruit-growing region of Motueka, the golden-sand beach of Kaiteriteri and north to Abel Tasman National Park. Nelson is renowned for its ceramic and glass artists and particularly, for wearable art. It is a city of artists and artisans, festivals and markets, lovingly-restored historic houses, a warm climate and good coffee.

Mapua, Tasman Bay.

Sunrise on Tasman Bay.

Sunset on Tasman Bay.

Nelson Cathedral.

BELOW: Pelorus River.

Mural, Nelson waterfront.

Aerial view of Nelson.

Cloudy Bay vineyard.

Governors Bay, Queen Charlotte Sound.

Outdoor enthusiasts also mill into Nelson over summer, the gateway to many northern tramping tracks and National Parks. There is little closer to Paradise than the clear waters lapping the white granite sands of Abel Tasman National Park. So deep is the water on its coast that ferries bringing trampers and day trippers to the sun-filled beaches reverse in and lower their gangways straight onto the sand. Kayakers mosey around shell banks and forest edges. Bird and fishlife abounds.

Nearby Kahurangi National Park, established in 1996, is one of New Zealand's newest and largest and extends right through to the west coast. There is only one road through to Golden Bay, Farewell Spit and the northern west coast and that is via the notoriously steep and winding Takaka Hill. Marble cut from the hills of Takaka provided the building blocks of Nelson's Cathedral.

On the Nelson side of Takaka Hill, near Riwaka, are the Pupu Springs. Clear clean water gushes from a chasm in the ground, part of an extensive artesian kaast limestone and cave landscape. So clear is the water that a periscope allows visitors to see 70 metres down into a rippling underwater wonder-world of colourful aquatic weeds and changing lights.

Anakiwa, Queen Charlotte Sound.

The township of Picton.

65

Kaikoura.

Castle Hill near Arthurs Pass.

New Zealand fur seal.

CANTERBURY

Early European settlers immediately saw the agricultural potential of the vast alluvial plains of Canterbury and of the foothills of the nearby Alps. Sheep soon dotted the high country and ears of wheat and grains swayed on the plains. Christchurch, near the port of Lyttelton, grew quickly as more and more sailing ships arrived, bringing colonists seeking their agrarian Arcadia. The city fathers designed a town essentially English in character, built with the stone and brick clays so easily accessible in the foothills and plains. Today beautiful nineteenth-century buildings form the heritage base of the city we now call the Garden City.

Magnificent braided rivers of the Canterbury Plains, such as the Waimakariri, Rakaia and Rangitata Rivers, begin their journey in the glaciers, lakes and mountain streams of the Southern Alps. Gathering glacial rock on their way they tumble it round, then dump it on the lowlands to form the dramatic ever-moving pebble banks of the long river deltas — favoured haunts of trout fishers and jet-boaters. The State-Highway-1 bridge that crosses the Rakaia River near the coast is New Zealand's longest at 1.8 kilometres.

Most of the towns of the plains have grown as service centres to the wide variety of vegetable and grain crops that jigsaw the countryside. Irrigation ditches and spray pumps tend grain plants as they change from new green to mature golden brown and grass plants that feed the increasing number of dairy farms in the region.

Lake Ruataniwha.

Punting on the Avon River, Christchurch.

To the north of the Canterbury Plains the Kaikoura Ranges rise to over 2000 metres and drop eastwards to the sea. Two of the most scenic roads and railways in the country wind around the jagged coastal edge, both forced, at times, through headland tunnels. On the coastal rocks fur seals bask in the sun or surf spray and, offshore, tourist boats go in search of whales and dolphins. The town of Kaikoura is famous for its seafood, its Maori name meaning 'meal of crayfish' (koura — crayfish, kai — food). Now, too, local wines make the local seafood delicacies even more appetising. Local art reflects the delightful vagaries of the coast.

Early Maori doggedly made their way westwards over the Alps in search of greenstone (pounamu). Today there are only three roads that traverse the Main Divide — at Lewis Pass and Arthurs Pass (from Canterbury) and Haast Pass (from Southland). Lewis Pass runs deep into forested mountains between the Southern Alps and the Spencer Range, by-passing Hanmer Springs, a source of natural mineral waters that have long soothed many an aching limb.

Arthurs Pass is by far and away more dramatic, arguably

The Arts Centre, Christchurch.

the jewel in the crown of New Zealand road adventures. The road winds along the edge of the cold languorous braids of the Waimakariri River then up into the awesome glaciated high-country terraces of Craigieburn. Arthurs Pass township is at the top of the pass (about 920 metres), a chalet-style ski resort. Then, over the top, the road winds down the Otira Gorge on a magnificent viaduct structure — a wondrous piece of mountain engineering. The alternative is to cross the divide in the Trans Alpine train, on an equally scenic passenger and goods railway that disappears underground at Arthurs Pass through the 8.55-kilometre-long Otira Tunnel.

The hills of Banks Peninsula are the only high land in the east of Canterbury. They provide shelter to Lyttelton Harbour, Christchurch's main port. Here, beautiful nineteenth-century wooden houses blend with the more pragmatic structures of a busy maritime centre. On the southern side of the peninsula, the little gem of Akaroa — a town proud of its early French heritage, with street names such as Rue Lavaud and Rue Jolie and a remarkable collection of early French-style buildings — nestles into a crook of the picturesque Akaroa Harbour.

The Mt Cavendish gondola.

Hôtel des Pêcheurs at Duvauchelle, Banks Peninsula.

'Pancake rocks' at Punakaiki.

The Taramakau River.

WEST COAST

Land of mountain mist, lush rainforest, rugged coast and bright sunny days, the West Coast has the ability to touch your soul. Separated from the rest of the South Island by the majestic snow-capped Southern Alps, this isolated region between coast and mountain — 600 kilometres long and no more than 70 kilometres wide — is a spectacular natural heritage zone which remains a pioneer frontier.

Only 31,000 people live a distinctive culture of their own here, where hospitality and pioneering spirit combine. Several historic sites display the wonders of former gold-rush days. The mountain rivers were long the destination of Maori who searched for sacred 'pounamu' (nephrite jade or greenstone). Now, world-class literary and fine arts artists and craftspeople make the quiet natural wonderland of seashore, bird and fish life, pounamu, glaciers, lakes and forest their canvas of life and abode. Small towns, surviving on farming, coal mining and tourism, welcome travellers for a range of adventures. Quaint and high-class accommodation, cafés and restaurants, galleries and tourist sites cater for nature-tourism adventures such as tramping, mountaineering, scenic flights, caving, rafting, fishing, horse treks and jet-boating as well as glacier walks.

The coastal edge of the West Coast is a mix of rugged rock juxtaposed with isolated silent wetland lakes. At Punakaiki — a world-renowned tourist destination — curiously-layered stacks of rocks are pounded by Tasman Sea waves, blowholes spurt geyser-towers of water and massive kelp swirls in tempestuous cauldrons.

Downtown Hokitika.

Two visitors explore Franz Josef Glacier.

At Okarito, quiet waters are a major feeding ground for over 70 species of birds — the only known breeding ground of the beautiful white heron (kotuku).

In the centre of the coast is Hokitika. In March, each year, it is inundated with visitors when it hosts the Hokitika Wild Foods Festival. Gastronomic adventure seekers come from far and wide to experience new taste sensations, from roasted huhu grubs and sheep's testicles to wild berry conserves.

Further south, at the Franz Josef and Fox townships, visitors' expressions change to awe and wonder. Here, two of some 140 glaciers that flow from the Southern Alps reach the lowland forests, only 250 metres above sea level (the only place outside of Argentina where this occurs). It is an awesome experience to stand beside or on a massive tongue of ice, only a few kilometres from the townships, in a warm and mild climate. Guiding companies here offer glacier walks and climbing experiences for all ages and capabilities and heli-hikes and scenic flights are also popular.

Ten kilometres from the Fox village is tiny Lake Matheson sheltered from wind and often totally calm. In its reflections

Sunrise on Fox Glacier.

are New Zealand's highest mountain peaks, Aoraki/Mount Cook and Mount Tasman. So still can the lake become at dawn and in the dusk, it is often difficult to tell whether a photo taken at this time is up the right way or not.

Equally beautiful is the wetland country of the southern West Coast. It is estimated that only two per cent of the kahikatea forests that once spread over much of the country remain in South Westland. New Zealand fur seals breed on the coastal rocks and at Jackson's Head there is a breeding colony of Fiordland crested penguin. Hector's dolphin are seen off the beaches.

Haast township is on the edge of the Haast River. This, the Southern Alps' lowest mountain pass, was used by Maori in search of pounamu and, for a century, packhorses and cattle crossed the divide here. It wasn't until 1965 that State Highway 6 finally connected the West Coast to Wanaka, passing through magnificent rugged inclines where rainfall is heavy and regular, and torrents of water rush alongside the road and under bridges. Some 300,000 travellers pass through here each year.

Lake Matheson.

Lake Mapourika.

Lake Matheson.

THE SOUTHERN ALPS

The grandeur of the 550-kilometre-long Southern Alps permeates much of the scenery of the South Island. Along the rugged snowy backbone, massive glaciated peaks gable sheer gullies and hung lakes of ice. Only a few adventurers experience this celestial alpine world, but in the high-country foothills, riverside roadways wend their way into mountain passes and up to mountain lakes amongst scree slopes, bouldered rivers, glaciers and majestic peaks.

Nineteen peaks over 3000 metres are located centrally in the Aoraki/Mount Cook National Park, many of which can be seen from both sides of the divide. The park is part of Te Wahipounamu, South Westland World Heritage Area in recognition of its outstanding natural values. Glaciers cover 40 per cent of it. There is virtually no forest, but the rock and ice landscape is alive with wonderful alpine plants and mountain birds that thrive in wide-open spaces — kea, falcons and the well-camouflaged pipit.

In the high country, at the gateway to the national park, Lake Pukaki provides many a photo-perfect view of the Alps. New Zealand's highest peak, Aoraki/Mount Cook (3754 metres) stands tall and angular at the end of the lake.

LEFT: Mt Cook.

Church of the Good Shepherd, Lake Tekapo.

The Treble Cone Ski Field.

BELOW: Lakefront, Wanaka.

The high-country lakes are a uniquely beautiful soft turquoise in colour caused by powdered rock that flows into their waters, gouged and ground by mountain glaciers. The turquoise waters of Lake Tekapo, further south in the Mackenzie Country, are surrounded by a vast basin of golden tussock-land, protected from westerly weather by the Alps and the Two Thumb Range. Here, the unforgettable little stone 'Church of the Good Shepherd', isolated on the rocky banks of the lake, enjoys some of New Zealand's highest sunshine hours and low rainfall.

The tussock-lined road of the Lindis Pass at the south end of the Mackenzie District skirts through the Alps to Lake Wanaka, a lakeside resort near the Treble Cone ski fields. A nearby road winds up the river of the Matukituki, deep into a beech-forested alpine valley at the foot of the walking and mountain-climbing tracks of Mount Aspiring National Park — Mount Aspiring (3027 metres) is the only Southern Alp peak over 3000 metres not within the Aoraki/Mt Cook area. The spectacular road between Lake Wanaka and the Haast Pass through to Westland borders Lake Hawea, where

The Cardrona Hotel.

Lindis Pass.

An inhabitant of the high country — the kea.

Queenstown by night.

Trout fishing, Lake Wakatipu.

towering grey rock slopes plunge steeply into placid water.

Some of New Zealand's most popular ski slopes and tramping tracks are located in the mountains surrounding the South Island's largest lakes, Lake Te Anau and Lake Wakatipu, at the Fiordland end of the Southern Alps. Queenstown, on the banks of Wakatipu, is arguably the ski capital of the island. The nearby Remarkable Mountain Range is equally picturesque. A gondola ride above the town highlights the expansive views while the SS *Earnslaw*, an historic steam vessel, plies the waters and a vintage steam train, the Kingston Flyer, runs at the lake's southern reaches. This town and many others are launching pads for adventure seekers wanting to ski, heli-ski, jet-boat, bungy-jump, canyon-walk, mountain-climb, or simply walk some of our scenic mountain/forest tracks. The Rees and Dart River Tracks begin at the northern reaches of Lake Wakatipu, each of them climbing through native beech forest and along subalpine snowlines, an alternative access to Mount Aspiring National Park. Jet-boaters and white-water rafters look for thrills and excitement on the wild and untamed waters of the Shotover River.

The Shotover Jet, Queenstown.

Autumn in Arrowtown.

Paragliding, Queenstown.

Winegrowing in the Gibbston Valley.

BELOW: Sunset, Central Otago.

Alexandra.

It is a world-renowned joke that New Zealand is home to more sheep than people. In Central Otago those ratios are dramatically true. About 11,000 square kilometres of hill country have fewer than 16,000 permanent residents. Romney, Corriedale, English Leicester and other sheep breeds, alongside world-boutique-market fine-wool Merinos, wander the high-country stations.

The rolling hills of Central Otago are a landscape of idyll and timelessness, repeating rises of tussock grassland fold in and out of shadow; one day sharply defined, another day soft and fluid. First revered by adventurers and settlers chasing dreams of riches in gold, the hills were cut into, tunnelled, sluiced, and scattered with tailings. Since, their curves and nuances have been immortalised by artists such as Colin McCahon and Grahame Sydney.

Most inland towns are nestled alongside rivers where small protected micro-climates nurture stone-fruit trees such as cherries and apricots, that grow best between temperatures of 10°C and 30°C. Cold weather makes for crisp clear days. On surrounding hills, wildflowers and thyme make colourful displays. Nearby, pebbled alluvial river plains are ideal for grape growing and many world-class wines are proudly produced.

Like most Otago towns, Cromwell is surrounded by vibrant foliage in autumn. The friendly township has a strong local heritage of gold panning and mining and thrives on an orchard economy. Along with Clyde

Autumn trees, Central Otago.

BELOW: Blue Lake, St Bathans.

and Roxburgh on the mighty Clutha River — New Zealand's largest by volume — it is also one of several Otago townships built or redeveloped to support the establishment of hydro-electric dams and power stations.

At Oamaru, an east-coast town with a vista over the vast Pacific Ocean, the townspeople are proud of their Victorian heritage. Frequently, locals dress in Victorian costume to celebrate and highlight the town's beautiful nineteenth-century buildings constructed of Oamaru stone. A blue penguin colony can be visited on the coast nearby and further south, large fascinating spherical concretion rocks lie on a sandy beach at Moeraki.

Natural beauty looms large on the Otago Peninsula. Predominantly of volcanic origin, the peninsula is steep and rugged on the Pacific side. Here, at Taiaroa Head, is the world's only mainland breeding colony of royal albatross. Young fledglings launch themselves from the cliffs to follow a wandering life over Pacific waves.

Inside the peninsula, a 20-kilometre-long shallow-bottomed fiord provides a warm sheltered harbour, alive with sea and

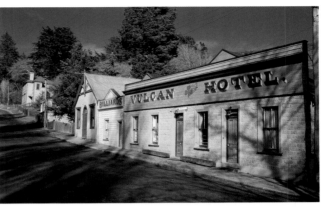

The Vulcan Hotel, St Bathans.

Moeraki boulders, North Otago.

Dunedin by night.

A royal albatross.

St Kilda Beach, Dunedin.

birdlife, including the endangered yellow-eyed penguin, seals, Hooker's sea lions and the occasional sea elephant. They are all an easy drive from Otago's main city of Dunedin.

Originally founded by whalers and gold miners, Dunedin developed quickly when colonised by early Scottish settlers. New Zealand's first refrigerated cargo of meat for England left Port Chalmers on SS *Dunedin* in 1882 establishing the peninsula as a thriving primary-produce service port and Dunedin as a wealthy town. Its famous stone cathedral rises above the Octagon, the main central city 'square'. Now, Dunedin is renowned as a university city flooded by 'Scarfies' each academic year, and as a city of cafés and bars, music and fashion.

A trip to Dunedin is not complete without an exploration of the Catlins — a region of stunning landform, flora and fauna on the south-easternmost coast of the South Island. At Curio Bay a 180-million-year-old fossilised forest is of international geological significance. There are also wonderful views of the Cathedral Caves, and, at Nugget Point, of penguins and seals of many species. Waterfalls and lighthouses also make up part of the varied landscape.

Matai Falls, the Catlins.

Milford Sound.

Te Anau countryside.

The *Lady Bowen*, Milford Sound.

Near the Homer Tunnel in winter.

SOUTHLAND

The southernmost districts of New Zealand bask in a glorious isolation which has never stopped people visiting or settling. On the far western side of the South Island, however, a vast wilderness of native bush, rugged mountains and wind-whipped coast remains unpenetrated by roads. Fiordland National Park is the largest in New Zealand and one of the largest in the world. Here, original beech and podocarp rainforest is the undisturbed home to most bird species of New Zealand, as well as many no longer seen elsewhere in the country. The wild west coast is fingered by fourteen 400-metre-deep glaciated fiords. Most of them are accessible only by sea.

Milford Sound and Doubtful Sound are the only exceptions. Doubtful Sound can be accessed by road, but only after a boat trip across Lake Manapouri. Milford Sound — the destination of walkers on the world-famous Milford Track — is reached through the Homer Tunnel road at the northern end of Lake Te Anau. High rainfall and a series of dramatic waterfalls make the sounds a unique marine environment. A permanent layer of fresh water on the surface of the salt water, mixed with tannins from the vegetation on land, forms a murky layer which cuts down the light penetrating the salt water. As a result, in the top salt layers there are many distinct species of tropical fish, corals, sponges and brachiopods (clam-like creatures that have remained unchanged for over 300 million years). The fiords support one of the world's largest colonies of black coral.

Mitre Peak in mist, Milford Sound.

Eglinton Valley, Fiordland.

Lake Gunn, Fiordland.

Inland, Lake Te Anau is the South Island's largest lake and Te Anau town is a centre for tourism, water sports, tramping and mountaineering. The Milford, Routeburn, Hollyford and Kepler tracks are all accessed via Te Anau. The road from Te Anau to Milford Sound is one of the country's most beautiful. Wandering through golden tussock-land of the Eglinton Valley it passes by hanging valleys, terraces and repeating fans of scree.

The more easterly part of Southland moves into rolling hills rather than rugged mountains. Fishing communities haul up blue cod, orange roughy, mullet and the far-famed fleshy Bluff oyster. Brown and rainbow trout and salmon in the rivers, sheep and beef on the hills and a wide variety of locally grown fruits including apricots, cherries and wine grapes provide for export and the local market.

Southland too was settled mainly by Scots and a local pronunciation with rolled 'rrrs' persists today. Invercargill City has remained much the same as it was when it developed in the late nineteenth and early twentieth centuries. Original Victorian buildings of stone and timber run cheek by jowl through the centre alongside large established private and

A yellow-eyed penguin chick.

Tay Street, Invercargill.

St Marys Basilica from Otepuni Gardens, Invercargill.

The signpost at Stirling Point, Bluff.

public gardens. The attraction of a recently-established 'no fees' institute of technology is revitalising the city. It is the home of winning netball teams, and a flamboyant mayor is putting a once-forgotten city strongly back on the national map and psyche.

The southernmost town of the South Island, Bluff is an archetypal fishing town. Here you can buy oysters, lobsters, paua and fish directly from the processing plants. Fishing boats linger at the wharfside. A signpost at Stirling Point proudly announces its southern status as the beginning of State Highway 1 and emblazons distances to London, New York, Tokyo, as well as to Stewart Island 35 kilometres across Foveaux Strait.

For anyone seeking peace and tranquillity, Stewart Island — the smallest of New Zealand's three main islands — is the ultimate destination. Clear clean waters make it a snorkelling and diving paradise. Human settlement and roads are confined to a small area on the north-east coast and the rest is a natural forested wilderness area with a spectacular indented coastline.

The view from Bluff Hill.

Sunrise, Halfmoon Bay, Stewart Island.

Boatsheds, Halfmoon Bay, Stewart Island.

Thule, Paterson Inlet, Stewart Island.

Lonnekers Beach, Halfmoon Bay, Stewart Island.

Mike Hollman Photography
P.O. Box 331 662, Takapuna
Auckland, New Zealand
www.mikehollman.com

National Library of New Zealand Cataloguing-in-Publication Data
Hollman, Mike.
Spectacular New Zealand : through the lens of Mike Hollman /
[photography by] Mike Hollman ; text by Sue Hall. 1st ed.
ISBN 1-86971-045-2
1. New Zealand—Description and travel. 2. New
Zealand—Description and travel—Pictorial works. I. Hall, Sue,
1951- II. Title.
919.30440222—dc 22

A Hodder Moa Book
Published in 2005 by Hachette Livre NZ Ltd
4 Whetu Place, Mairangi Bay
Auckland, New Zealand

Designed and produced by Hachette Livre NZ Ltd
Printed by Everbest Printing Ltd, China

Cover photograph: Lake Tekapo